OECD Development Policy Tools

How to Select Buyers of Oil, Gas and Minerals

GUIDANCE FOR STATE-OWNED ENTERPRISES

This work is published under the responsibility of the Secretary-General of the OECD. The opinions expressed and arguments employed herein do not necessarily reflect the official views of the member countries of the OECD or its Development Centre.

This document, as well as any data and map included herein, are without prejudice to the status of or sovereignty over any territory, to the delimitation of international frontiers and boundaries and to the name of any territory, city or area.

Please cite this publication as:
OECD (2020), *How to Select Buyers of Oil, Gas and Minerals: Guidance for State-Owned Enterprises*, OECD Development Policy Tools, OECD Publishing, Paris, *https://doi.org/10.1787/a522e6c0-en*.

ISBN 978-92-64-43828-6 (print)
ISBN 978-92-64-83822-2 (pdf)

OECD Development Policy Tools
ISSN 2518-6248 (print)
ISSN 2518-3702 (online)

Photo credits: Cover design by Aida Buendía (OECD Development Centre) based on images from © Der_Wolf/Shutterstock.com.

Corrigenda to publications may be found on line at: *www.oecd.org/about/publishing/corrigenda.htm*.
© OECD 2020

The use of this work, whether digital or print, is governed by the Terms and Conditions to be found at *http://www.oecd.org/termsandconditions*.

Foreword

At the 2016 Anti-Corruption Summit held in May 2016, general consensus emerged among countries that made commitments on commodity trading transparency around the need for the OECD to host and convene an international dialogue on commodity trading transparency to identify and address existing gaps for improved resource governance and to effectively advance the transparency agenda.

Sales of publicly-owned oil, gas and minerals are of particular economic significance to the budgets of developing countries due to the scale of those revenues. Research by the Natural Resource Governance Institute (NRGI) in respect of oil and gas sales from state-owned enterprises (SOEs) to commodity traders and other buyers, showed that sales from 35 SOEs generated over USD 1.5 trillion in 2016 (Malden and Williams, 2019[1]). However, very few governments or SOEs have published data on the process to select buyers of oil, gas and minerals, with contextual information to understand how decisions are made and the various procedures used.

The risks of corruption in the selection of buyers of publicly-owned commodities is significant due to the large volume of commodities sold and the amount of money involved. The establishment of rigorous and robust processes and criteria for the selection of buyers can help to reduce the political pressure to use discretion (whether in terms of pricing or arbitrariness of selection), especially considering the potential for involvement of politically exposed persons (PEPs) in the transaction.

Therefore, getting the buyer selection process right is a crucial step to prevent potential public revenue losses that can arise through sub-optimal allocation and corruption. This document sets out guidance on transparent and competitive processes for selecting buyers can help host governments and SOEs to reduce discretion, close opportunities for corruption, favouritism and public rent diversion that would result in public revenue losses. This guidance may also be used by government agencies that market commodities on behalf of the state and is also applicable to domestic markets. The focus of this document is on conventional sales (spot sales, term sale agreements) of oil, gas and minerals.

The development of this Guidance was undertaken under the auspices of the Thematic Dialogue on Commodity Trading Transparency – a multi-stakeholder platform established in response to the call received from the 2016 Anti-Corruption Summit and in line with the high-level mandate received from the Governing Board of the OECD Development Centre on 3 October 2017 (Governing Board of the OECD Development Centre, 2017[2]).

This Guidance complements the work of the EITI that seeks to improve transparency around commodity sales transactions from both a seller and buyer perspective. Requirement 4.2 b) of the 2019 EITI Standard provides that:

> *implementing countries including state-owned enterprises are encouraged to disclose a description of the process for selecting the buying companies, the technical and financial criteria used to make the selection, the list of selected buying companies, any material deviations from the applicable legal and regulatory framework governing the selection of buying companies, and the related sales agreements (EITI, 2019[3]).*

Furthermore, this guidance reflects the provisions laid out in the EITI *Guidance Note 26: Reporting on first trades in oil*, that recommends the disclosure of a description of the process for selecting the buying companies and the technical and financial criteria used to make the selection. (EITI, 2017[4]).

Acknowledgements

This Guidance was prepared by Elliot Smith, Legal Analyst, Natural Resources for Development Unit, OECD Development Centre under the guidance, direction and supervision of Lahra Liberti, Head of the Natural Resources for Development Unit, OECD Development Centre. This Guidance was developed within the framework of the OECD Development Centre's Policy Dialogue on Natural Resource-based Development, and in particular its Thematic Dialogue on Commodity Trading Transparency. The Guidance was prepared in response to the demand received from the participants in the Ninth Plenary Meeting of the Policy Dialogue on Natural Resource-based Development to work towards the development of guidance to support state-owned enterprises in selecting buyers.

The Guidance was developed through an iterative process, involving SOEs, from both EITI and non-EITI countries, selling oil, gas and minerals, as well as other stakeholders from governments, the private sector and civil society.

The Guidance benefitted from the input of these stakeholders during discussions on early drafts of the document at the Eleventh Plenary Meeting of the Policy Dialogue on Natural Resource-based Development held on 12-13 December 2018, the Twelfth Plenary Meeting of the Policy Dialogue on Natural Resource-based Development held on 20-21 June 2019, and the Fourteenth Plenary Meeting of the Policy Dialogue on Natural Resource-based Development, held on 26 June 2020.

Additional input was received from respondents to a *Questionnaire to State-owned Enterprises on Selection Procedures used to Select Buyers of Oil, Gas and Minerals* from August to October 2018, as well as comments on the final draft Guidance from SOEs and other interested stakeholders received from July to August 2020.

Comments received from key stakeholders participating in the Policy Dialogue – state-owned enterprises, resource-rich countries, commodity trading companies, civil society and international organisations – are gratefully acknowledged. In particular, the author is thankful to the Extractive Industries Transparency Initiative (EITI); Ghana National Petroleum Corporation (GNPC); Natural Resource Governance Institute (NRGI); Nigerian National Petroleum Corporation (NNPC); Okavango Diamond Company (ODC); and U4 Anti-Corruption Resource Centre for their valuable contributions.

The author would also like to thank OECD colleagues Hans Christiansen and Alison McMeekin (OECD Directorate for Financial and Enterprise Affairs) for their expert review and valuable comments, and Delphine Grandrieux and Elizabeth Nash (OECD Development Centre) for support during the publication process.

Table of contents

Foreword 3

Acknowledgements 5

1. Putting in place institutional arrangements 8
   1.1. Corporate governance of SOEs 8
      1.1.1. Role of the SOE Board 10
      1.1.2. Auditing arrangements 11
   1.2. Establishing a mandate to sell publicly-owned commodities 11
   1.3. Establishing and resourcing the buyer selection team 12
      1.3.1. Mandate and procedural requirements 13
      1.3.2. Conflicts of interest 13
      1.3.3. Composition and capability 14
      1.3.4. Oversight and reporting 14

2. Designing the buyer selection process 16
   2.1. Reducing discretion in the buyer selection process 16
   2.2. Determining the type of contractual arrangement 16
      2.2.1. Spot sales 17
      2.2.2. Term sale arrangements 17
      2.2.3. Commodity-for-product swap agreements 17
      2.2.4. Resource-backed finance agreements 18
      2.2.5. Government-to-government sales 19
   2.3. Determining the allocation method for buyer selection 19
      2.3.1. Direct negotiation with buyer 20
      2.3.2. Competitive selection 22
   2.4. Setting out the terms of the buyer selection process 25
      2.4.1. Pre-qualification process 25
      2.4.2. Pre-defined criteria to select buyers 26
   2.5. Establishing a pricing policy 30
      2.5.1. Overview 30
      2.5.2. Use of a commodity benchmark 31
      2.5.3. Transparency of pricing information 32
      2.5.4. Pricing adjustment mechanism in long-term sales agreements 32
   2.6. Drafting the contractual provisions 33

3. Carrying out the buyer selection process 35
   3.1. Proactive transparency measures 35
      3.1.1. Transparency of the SOE's sales policy 36
      3.1.2. Disclosure of the buyer selection criteria 37
      3.1.3. Disclosure of the commodity sales contract or its key terms 38
      3.1.4. Disclosure of the identity of buyers 38
      3.1.5. Disclosure of the buyers' beneficial ownership information 38
   3.2. Undertaking due diligence on buyers 39
      3.2.1. Beneficial ownership and involvement of politically exposed persons 41
      3.2.2. Conflicts of interest 43
      3.2.3. Additional due diligence requirements 43

3.3. Countering public rent diversion at point of revenue collection 44
Annex 46
References 47

Tables

Table 1.1. Ownership of commodities sold by selected SOEs 12
Table 2.1. Weighting criteria used in the buyer selection process by GNPC 29

Boxes

Box 1.1. What governments can do to promote integrity and anti-corruption in SOEs 8
Box 1.2. What SOEs can do to put together an effective buyer selection team 12
Box 1.3. What SOEs can do to identify and manage conflicts of interest in the buyer selection team. 14
Box 2.1. What SOEs can do to reduce discretion in the buyer selection process 16
Box 2.2. What SOEs and governments can do to reduce opacity in the bidding process 19
Box 2.3. What SOEs can do to reduce corruption risk in direct negotiations 21
Box 2.4. What SOEs can do to reduce risks of bid rigging in a competitive selection process 22
Box 2.5. What SOEs can do to detect bid rigging in a competitive selection process 24
Box 2.6. Financial information required by NNPC at the pre-qualification stage 27
Box 2.7. What SOEs can do to reduce corruption risks associated with local participation 28
Box 2.8. What SOEs can do to prevent losses associated with commodity mispricing 30
Box 2.9. Pricing policy for the sale of crude oil by NNPC 31
Box 2.10. What SOEs can do to reduce risks associated with unbalanced contractual provisions 33
Box 3.1. What SOEs can do to increase transparency and accountability in their commodity sales
  transactions 35
Box 3.2. Sales policy for the sale of crude oil by PMI 36
Box 3.3. What SOEs can do to undertake effective due diligence on buyers 39
Box 3.4. Information required from buyers prior to entering into negotiations to purchase crude oil
  from Petrotrin 40
Box 3.5. FATF Definition of politically exposed persons 41
Box 3.6. Red flags that may indicate corruption risks associated with BOs and involvement of
  PEPs 42
Box 3.7. OECD Definition of conflict of interest 43
Box 3.8. What SOEs and governments can do to counter public rent diversion 44

1. Putting in place institutional arrangements

1.1. Corporate governance of SOEs

> **Box 1.1. What governments can do to promote integrity and anti-corruption in SOEs**
>
> - Clearly define the rationale for state ownership, and clarify the objectives of individual SOEs;
>
> - Separate the state-owned sector's administration and regulation functions;
>
> - Encourage SOEs to establish internal controls, ethics and compliance measures, for instance in the form of an anti-corruption programme, that are based on risk assessments and that have their content and implementation subject to independent review;
>
> - The role of SOE boards should be clearly defined in relevant legislation including company law, regulations, the government ownership policy and corporate charters. Politicians who are in a position to influence materially the operating conditions of SOEs should not serve on their boards. An appropriate number of independent members should be on each board and sit on specialised committees (e.g. audit, risk management, remuneration);
>
> - Establish a disclosure policy that requires SOEs to consistently report in accordance with high quality internationally recognised standards on corporate disclosure and encourage that it is made publicly available. Disclosure requirements could include information related to the ownership, governance, operations, and financial results of SOEs including for example, pricing policies, costs, revenue flows, tax payments, financial flows between the SOE and the state, procurement plans, shareholders, SOE beneficial ownership, and disclosure of the identities of the SOE's major contractors and partners, including the beneficial ownership of such entities) (OECD, 2005[5]);
>
> - Encourage SOEs to develop efficient internal audit procedures and require that SOEs be subject to independent external audit based on international standards (OECD, 2005[5]);
>
> - Encourage participatory monitoring and other independent oversight mechanisms separate from state regulatory authorities (e.g. civil society and/ or parliamentary committees and courts) (OECD, 2016[5]);
>
> - Disclose all financial support by the state to SOEs in a transparent and consistent fashion (OECD, 2019[6]);
>
> - Clarify and make publicly available information about the ownership structure, including linking the SOEs to the ownership entity responsible for said SOEs. This could include recording SOEs in beneficial ownership registers; and

> - Encourage disclosure of the organisational structure of the SOE, including its subsidiaries and any joint ventures and the percentage owned in each such subsidiary/holding, as well as the countries of their incorporation and operation.

Before developing a buyer selection process or entering into direct negotiations with a potential buyer, SOEs and governments should ensure that appropriate and robust governance structures are in place to empower the SOE to undertake its operations (including buyer selection) in an efficient and transparent manner.

Robust governance arrangements for SOEs are particularly important for mitigating the heightened corruption risk in the extractive sector. According to a 2018 OECD study, SOEs in the oil and gas and mining sectors are more likely to have reported experiencing corruption or other irregular practices (deviations from integrity that harm SOEs and that open avenues for specific forms of corruption, including bribery) than SOEs in other sectors. These risks include: interference in decision-making processes, favouritism (nepotism, cronyism and patronage), undeclared conflicts of interest, stealing or theft of goods from the company, fraud and receiving bribes (OECD, 2018[7]).

In recognition of the important role that SOEs can play in the economy, the OECD developed in 2005 (and revised in 2015) the *Guidelines on Corporate Governance of State-Owned Enterprises* (Corporate Governance Guidelines) which provide recommendations to governments on how to ensure that SOEs can operate with similar efficiently, transparency and accountability as good practice private enterprises. They are supported by the *OECD Guidelines on Anti-Corruption and Integrity in State-Owned Enterprises (2019)*. The Corporate Governance Guidelines recommend that governments should develop an ownership policy. The policy should inter alia define the overall rationales for state ownership, the state's role in the governance of SOEs, how the state will implement its ownership policy, and the respective roles and responsibilities of those government departments involved in its implementation. The state should define the rationales for owning individual SOEs, such as national oil companies (NOCs) or national mining companies (NMCs), and subject these enterprises to recurrent review. Any public policy objectives that individual SOEs, or groups of SOEs, are required to achieve should be clearly mandated by the relevant authorities and disclosed (OECD, 2015[8]).

Governments should allow SOEs full operational autonomy to achieve their defined objectives and refrain from intervening in SOE management. Often, strict separation between ownership and other government functions may not be in place or effective, and therefore, the line between SOE operations and the interest of political figures may be blurred.

Where SOEs combine economic activities and public policy objectives, high standards of transparency and disclosure regarding their cost and revenue structures must be maintained, allowing for an attribution to main activity areas. As a guiding principle, SOEs undertaking economic activities should not be exempt from the application of general laws, tax codes and regulations (OECD, 2015[8]).

In some circumstances, SOEs sell commodities on behalf of the state as opposed to selling commodities on their own account as a commercial entity. SOEs should be clear in their reporting and disclosures which transactions are attributable to both commercial and non-commercial objectives.

Clarity around ownership and governance structures of key actors involved in commodity trading is of particular importance in situations where private actors play a role alongside the government. For example, many SOEs are 100% government owned. However, some may be partially listed on a stock exchange, such as Equinor in Norway or Petrobras in Brazil, or may be partially privately owned, such as Debswana in Botswana.

In situations where the state is not the sole owner, the state and SOEs should ensure that all shareholders are treated equitably. SOEs should develop an active policy of communication and consultation with all shareholders, and transactions between the state and SOEs, and between SOEs, should take place on market consistent terms (OECD, 2015[8]).

SOEs should report material financial and non-financial information on the enterprise in line with high quality internationally recognised standards of corporate disclosure, and including areas of significant concern for the state as an owner and the general public (OECD, 2015[8]).

Persons willing to report real or encouraged illegal or irregular practices in and concerning SOEs, including related to the state owner, should be offered protection in law and practice against all types of unjustified treatments as a result of reporting. Transparent procedures should be developed to ensure that all detected irregularities, in and concerning SOEs are investigated and prosecuted when necessary in accordance with domestic legal procedures. Enforcement of provisions in the legal framework should be rigorous and systematic, and ensure that SOEs are not given unfair advantage or protected by their ownership (OECD, 2019[6]).

1.1.1. Role of the SOE Board

The boards of SOEs should have the necessary authority, competencies and objectivity to carry out their functions of strategic guidance and monitoring of management. The role of SOE boards should be clearly defined in relevant legislation, including company law.

The state should let SOE boards exercise their responsibilities and should respect their independence. The boards of SOEs should develop, implement, monitor and communicate internal controls, ethics and compliance programmes or measures, including those which contribute to preventing fraud and corruption. They should be based on country norms, in conformity with international commitments and apply to the SOE and its subsidiaries. SOEs should observe high standards of responsible business conduct. Expectations established by the government in this regard should be communicated to SOE boards and publicly disclosed, with mechanisms for their implementation that are clearly established (OECD, 2015[8]).

The process of nomination of individuals to SOE boards should be transparent, clearly structured and based on an appraisal of the variety of skills, competencies and experiences required. Board members should be selected, among other things, on the basis of personal integrity and professional qualification (OECD, 2019[6]). Competence and experience requirements should derive from an evaluation of the incumbent board and needs related to the SOE's long term strategy.

The boards of SOEs should be assigned clear mandates and ultimate responsibility for the SOE's performance. Mechanisms should be implemented to avoid conflicts of interest preventing board members from objectively carrying out their board duties and to limit political interference in board processes (OECD, 2015[8]). Politicians who are in a position to influence materially the operating conditions of SOEs should not serve on their boards. Persons linked directly with the executive powers – i.e. heads of state, heads of government and ministers – should not serve on boards as this may cast serious doubts on the independence of their judgment.

Civil servants and other public officials can serve on boards under the condition that qualification and conflict of interest requirements for board members apply equally to them. A pre-determined "cooling-off" period should as a general rule be applied to former politicians (OECD, 2019[6]).

To enhance the objectivity of SOE boards a certain minimum number of independent board members on SOE boards should be required – that is, independent from the state and from the enterprise. Independent board members should be free of any material interests or relationships with the enterprise, its management or its ownership that could jeopardise the exercise of objective judgement. Full transparency surrounding board member qualifications is especially important for SOEs.

It should be a board responsibility to appoint and remove the CEO, not the state owner's (OECD, 2015[8]). The state should expect that boards apply high standards for hiring and conduct of top management and other members of executive management who should also be appointed based on professional criteria (OECD, 2019[6]).

1.1.2. Auditing arrangements

SOEs should be subject to robust and regular auditing processes that consist of internal audits within the SOE as well as and external audit by third parties and, additionally where the legal framework allows, by the state audit institute.

In terms of internal auditing, SOEs should develop efficient internal audit procedures and establish an internal audit function that is monitored by and reports directly to the board and to the audit committee or the equivalent corporate organ.

The state body responsible for exercising ownership rights on behalf of the state should receive all necessary and relevant information from the SOE in a timely manner, in order to regularly assess SOE performance, and oversee their compliance with applicable corporate governance standards.

Governments should ensure that SOEs are subject to external audits that are carried out in accordance with internationally recognised standards. Adequate procedures should be developed for the selection of external auditors and it is crucial that they are independent from SOE management as well as from the government (OECD, 2015[8]). When supreme audit institutions play a role in monitoring SOEs, the state should require that SOEs be additionally subject to annual external audits that are carried out in accordance with internationally recognised standards (OECD, 2019[6]).

1.2. Establishing a mandate to sell publicly-owned commodities

SOEs should ensure that they have the legal mandate to enter into sale and purchase agreements with buyers to sell publicly-owned commodities. Governments may grant authority to SOEs to enter into commodity sale agreements, and this authority should be clearly conferred by law, statutes, presidential or ministerial decree. In other cases, the ownership rights (title) of the commodity may be vested in the SOE.

In some circumstances, SOEs may sell commodities on behalf of the state, and in other circumstances may sell commodities on their own account as a commercial entity. It is not unusual for an SOE to sell commodities on both accounts – that is, acting on mixed objectives.

The ownership of the commodities sold by SOEs varies across countries. The majority of SOEs surveyed by the OECD Development Centre in 2018 reported that the SOE held the legal ownership of the commodities after the title to those commodities had been transferred from the state. In some cases, the state retains legal ownership and in other cases, legal ownership can be split between the SOE and the state. In Myanmar, the majority of gemstones sold by Myanmar Gems Enterprise (MGE) are owned directly by the government. In Suriname, commodities are owned directly by the SOE Staatsolie. Ownership of commodities is transferred from the state to Staatsolie once the crude oil has been processed. In Mongolia, ownership is transferred from the state to Erdenes Tavan Tolgoi (ETT) once the coal has been extracted by ETT.

In all cases, the SOE should have a clear mandate to enter into sale and purchase agreements with buyers.

Table 1.1. Ownership of commodities sold by selected SOEs

Country	SOE	Ownership of commodities
Colombia	Ecopetrol	SOE
Ghana	GNPC	SOE and government
Mexico	PMI Comercio Internacional (PMI)	SOE
Mongolia	Erdenes Tavan Tolgoi (ETT)	SOE and government
Mozambique	Empresa Nacional de Hidrocarbonetos (ENH)	SOE and government
Myanmar	MGE	SOE and government
Suriname	Staatsolie	SOE
Trinidad & Tobago	Petrotrin	SOE

Source: (OECD Development Centre, 2018[9]).

1.3. Establishing and resourcing the buyer selection team

> **Box 1.2. What SOEs can do to put together an effective buyer selection team**
>
> - Set clear parameters for the sale process (terms of reference, strategy, policy etc.);
> - Assemble a buyer selection team with multidisciplinary skills;
> - Strengthen the multidisciplinary skills of the team by hiring an external provider, if these skills cannot be located in-house;
> - Ensure that the buyer selection team operates autonomously from management and free from political interference but is still subject to a sufficient level of oversight at executive or board level; and
> - Ensure that there are clear reporting lines for employees to report concerns about real or encouraged illegal or irregular practices, and that reporting persons (whistle-blowers) are protected.

SOEs should create a team to undertake the buyer selection process and should ensure that this team is appropriately resourced to carry out its functions. The majority of the SOEs surveyed by the OECD Development Centre reported the existence of temporary or permanent teams to administer their buyer selection processes. These teams can be composed of and administrated solely by the SOE or can include representatives from other government agencies if required by law.

1.3.1. Mandate and procedural requirements

At the outset, and before any negotiations take place, it is important for senior leadership within the SOE (ideally at executive or board level) to set clear parameters for the sale process. These parameters should provide the buyer selection team with a clear mandate, which defines the scope for the sale process (including any negotiations), includes the terms of reference, powers and functions of the team, what is expected to be achieved, the elements that are subject to negotiation (and conversely those that are not), and the scope of the team's negotiating position in each of these areas.

SOEs should appoint a team leader who will be accountable to the senior leadership of the SOE (ideally at executive or board level), and will be required to establish that the buyer selection process accords with the mandate received, the parameters of the terms of reference, and any overarching selection strategy.

For example, in Ghana, for each buyer selection by Ghana National Petroleum Corporation (GNPC), senior management will first appoint an evaluation team. That team will then prepare the evaluation criteria and assess bids against that criteria. Subsequently, the evaluation team will submit a report on their findings and recommendations back to GNPC senior management who are empowered to make the final decision. At the end of each buyer selection process, the evaluation team is disbanded.

1.3.2. Conflicts of interest

Each member of the buyer selection team should be required to make a declaration of any conflict(s) of interest they may have with all bidders and potential buyers. A thorough assessment will be required for each declaration that identifies a conflict of interest to determine whether the conflict can be mitigated. Examples of potential mitigation measures include: divestment or liquidation of the interest by member of the buyer selection team (if applicable); resignation of the member from the conflicting private-capacity function (if applicable); recusal of the member from involvement in active decision making processes; and restriction of access by the member to particular information (OECD, 2003[10]).

If a conflict of interests cannot be mitigated, then that individual should not participate as a member of the buyer selection team.

> **Box 1.3. What SOEs can do to identify and manage conflicts of interest in the buyer selection team**
>
> - Identifying risks presented by bidders to the integrity of the SOE and its employees;
> - Prohibiting specific unacceptable forms of private interest;
> - Making employees aware of the circumstances in which conflicts can arise; and
> - Ensuring that effective procedures are deployed for the identification, disclosure, management, and promotion of the appropriate resolution of conflict-of-interest situations.
>
> *Source:* Adapted from (OECD, 2003[10]).

1.3.3. Composition and capability

Given the technical and commercial nature of the sales of oil, gas and minerals, SOEs may make use of multidisciplinary teams. Multidisciplinary skills that may be required are (but are not limited to): financial, commercial, technical, marketing, trading, due diligence, legal, procurement and risk management. In some cases, if these skills cannot be located in-house, they may need to be sourced from external organisations.

In some cases, buyer selection teams may involve other government agencies alongside the relevant SOE where required by law. In Albania, a "Commission" is responsible for overseeing the buyer selection process and evaluation of the bids. The Commission is comprised of three representatives from the Ministry of Infrastructure and Energy, two representatives from the SOE (Albpetrol), one representative from the State's Technical and Industrial Inspectorate, and one representative from the National Agency of Natural Resources (AKBN) (Deloitte, 2018[11]). In Mozambique, the buyer selection team has input from the SOE Empresa Nacional de Hidrocarbonetos (ENH), the Ministry of Mineral Resources and Energy, and the National Institute of Petroleum (INP).

1.3.4. Oversight and reporting

The buyer selection process is likely to attract substantial political interest and it may be difficult to shield the selection process from undue political influence. SOEs can seek to mitigate the risk of undue influence by establishing an autonomous buyer selection team with the corresponding mandate whilst also setting clear reporting lines and being subject to a sufficient level of oversight at executive or board level.

In Colombia, Ecopetrol has constituted a permanent team for the selection of buyers called the "International Trading Group" which is comprised of the: International Trade Manager, Head of Department of Crude Oil, Head of Department of Product and various individual traders. Another team, the "Commercial Committee" fulfils a review function of specific aspects of the buyer selection process. The Commercial Committee is comprised of the Commercial and Marketing Vice-Presidency, International Trade Manager, and the Commercial CFO. In Nigeria, bids are first evaluated against a set criteria, and then independent reports are compiled for NNPC Management by two separate teams: the NNPC Evaluation Team and the Nigerian Content Board.

SOEs should take appropriate steps to promote anti-corruption and integrity measures in their operations in order to encourage good governance and integrity, internal controls, ethics and compliance measures. In addition SOEs should set out clear rules and procedures for employees or other reporting persons to report concerns about real or encouraged illegal or irregular practices in or concerning SOEs (including subsidiaries or business partners). Reporting persons (also known as "whistle-blowers") should be protected in law and practice against all types of unjustified treatments as a result of reporting concerns (OECD, 2018[7]).

In Chile, Codelco's buyer selection team is subject to both internal audits and external audits carried out by government agencies. Ecopetrol (Colombia) and Pemex (Mexico) have established a whistle-blower line where personnel can use to report irregularities or concerns.

2. Designing the buyer selection process

2.1. Reducing discretion in the buyer selection process

> **Box 2.1. What SOEs can do to reduce discretion in the buyer selection process**
>
> - Set pre-determined and objective buyer selection criteria to be explicitly and transparently considered in the buyer selection processes;
> - Limit political interference in SOEs' technical decisions by making merit-based appointments. Invest in staff integrity and capacity and adopt strong employee accountability provisions;
> - Introduce standardised and automatic procedures (e.g. bid submission, revenue collection etc.) / develop standardised models or guidelines (e.g. contract terms); and
> - Set clear ethical standards and codes of conduct and provide certification and regular training for SOE employees in compliance-sensitive positions.
>
> *Source:* Adapted from (OECD, 2016[5]).

Discretionary power and a high politicisation of decision-making in the buyer selection process can result in significant public rent diversion. The discretionary power over decision-making held by both high and lower-ranking public officials is a major risk factor and undermines the effective prevention of corruption in the buyer selection process.

Discretionary decision making can result in the selection of buyer who may purchase the commodities for less than their market value, or who may not have the requisite financial and technical capacity to meet their obligations under a commodity sales contract. In practice, these 'unqualified' buyers are often intermediaries, who purport to act as the buyer in the transaction purchasing the commodity at a low price before quickly off-selling the commodity at a market price on the international market, without providing any logistical or other reasonable service. The buying company thus acts as a mere intermediary between the public entity or its marketing agent and a second-tier purchaser (OECD, 2016[5]).

2.2. Determining the type of contractual arrangement

SOEs will need to decide which type of contractual arrangement is most appropriate in their given context. The types of arrangements that are used to sell commodities need to be carefully considered due to the large amounts of financial flows involved and the corresponding potential high risk of corruption and public rent diversion.

There are several different methods that a SOE may use to select buyers of its oil, gas or mineral resources which can depend on strategic as well as economic factors. These arrangements may include: spot sales, term arrangements (short, medium and long-term) and government-to-government (G2G) transactions. Other factors that can influence the buyer selection process include: financing (resource-backed finance agreements); the procurement of products for the domestic market (commodity-for-product swap agreements); or the desire for a long-term relationship with an end user.

SOEs are not limited to the use of one type of contractual arrangement. For example, in Chile, Codelco uses both term sale agreements (80%) and spot sales (20%), whilst 5% of Codelco's sales are made using resource-backed finance agreements. In Ghana, GNPC uses both spot sales and term agreements for the sale of its crude. GNPC has two long-term agreements with Unipec Asia (15.5 years) and Litasco (5 years) to lift crude oil from GNPC's share of the Jubilee and TEN oil fields at a rate of approximately 5-8 lifting per year. If there is excess crude oil available after the liftings, GNPC will use the spot sales method to sell that additional crude oil (GHEITI, 2018[12]).

2.2.1. Spot sales

Spot sales are used by both NOCs and NMCs to select buyers for their oil, gas and minerals but are more common in sales of crude oil. Around a third of all sales of crude oil are made using this arrangement (Van Schaik, 2012[13]). Spot markets operate in real-time and can offer SOEs an instant sale and disposal of their commodities. Spot markets operate wherever the necessary infrastructure exists to conduct the transactions, and by using this method, SOEs will usually receive payment immediately or within a short time window.

Among the SOEs surveyed by the OECD Development Centre in 2018, several reported the use of spot sale arrangements. In Mexico, PMI reported that during the period 2015-17, 27% of the value of total export sales were made by spot sale method. Staatsolie reported 48% sales were made via this method and Ecopetrol reported that 58% of sales were sold via spot sales (OECD Development Centre, 2018[9]).

In order for SOEs to take advantage of the spot sale method, the necessary infrastructure should be in place to allow these sales. Furthermore the SOE will need a sophisticated trading desk to regularly monitor the market and position itself to be able to exploit the slightest supply disruption whilst avoiding demand weakness (Van Schaik, 2012[13]).

2.2.2. Term sale arrangements

Term sales refer to an arrangement where the SOE negotiates a contract with a buyer to supply a commodity over a longer time period, usually with a minimum of one year. The term arrangement will specify how the price will be determined, the total units of the commodity that will be sold, the point of delivery, and other contractual factors.

Term sale arrangements are used by SOEs to sell oil, gas and minerals, with around a two thirds of all crude oil sales sold via this method (Van Schaik, 2012[13]). In Mozambique, ENH sells the government's share of natural gas exclusively through term sale arrangements, usually for periods longer than ten years. In Colombia, in 2017, Ecopetrol sold 42% of the total value of its oil sales through term arrangements usually for a period of two years.

Term sale arrangements can provide SOEs with increased certainty and stability in regard to future revenue flows. SOEs should ensure that they are in a position to deliver on their supply obligations under a term sale arrangement, and have contingency plans in place to counter any disruption to supply.

2.2.3. Commodity-for-product swap agreements

Commodity-for-product swap agreements refer to an arrangement where an SOE 'swaps' commodities – usually crude oil, for other commodities – usually refined petroleum products. The past or current use of these swap agreements has been documented in Angola, China, Indonesia, Kuwait, Malaysia, Nigeria, Saudi Arabia and Venezuela.

These arrangements may be negotiated when the government is at a weak bargaining position, for example, when demand for their commodity is low or when they cannot pay cash for the refined products they require. Furthermore, since commodity-for-product swap agreements are highly context-specific, there are few industry standard terms or "best practices" against which to measure them – which makes undervaluation and mispricing difficult to identify.

Commodity-for-product swap agreements may offer opportunities for corruption and misappropriation of oil rents as suggested by large discrepancies observed between benchmark estimates and actual figures for government revenues in certain oil producing countries. The absence of money transfer and the secrecy surrounding contractual clauses make corrupt behaviours difficult to detect (OECD, 2016[5]).

The scale of commodities sold through commodity-for-product swap agreements can be quite significant. In Nigeria, between 2010 and 2014, NNPC sold oil worth USD 35 billion through one of these arrangements. In 2015, NNPC sold 210 000 barrels per day (which was one-tenth of Nigeria's entire production) through swap agreements. NRGI estimated a loss of USD 16 per barrel in public revenues due to unbalanced contract terms (Sayne, Gillies and Katsouris, 2015[14]).

Given the opacity of these arrangements and the opportunities for corruption and misappropriation, the use of commodity-for-product swap agreements should be carefully considered, to avoid the risk of underselling the resources.

2.2.4. Resource-backed finance agreements

Resource-backed finance agreements have become common over the last few decades, in particular for countries with limited access to capital and credit that use their resource wealth to secure financing. These can take the form of pre-payment or advance payment deals, where a government or SOE receives funds up-front in exchange for future resource production. Commodities can also be used to repay public sector debt, or used as collateral. The political pressure faced in some countries to spend commodity revenues quickly may lead to the negotiation of pre-payment arrangements granting favourable conditions to the buyer at the expense of the seller (e.g. discounted prices).

The disclosure of select information in respect of resource-backed finance agreements is required under the 2019 EITI Standard. Requirements 4.2.a and 4.3 require, at a minimum, disclosures on the terms of relevant agreements, parties involved, resources pledged, the value of the loan, and the volume and value of commodities exchanged (EITI, 2019[3]).

Whereas resource-backed finance agreements offer countries opportunities for access to finance, these loans also come with considerable risks, sometimes very onerous terms, and are not contracted on a competitive basis. Recent research by Public Eye illustrates how the use of resource-backed finance agreements can lead to significant public rent diversion (Public Eye, 2017[15]).

Governments may also under-value the country's future oil revenues in order to receive short-term injections of cash, often for political reasons. Furthermore, these agreements are frequently non-transparent to citizens, and off the government budget. Sometimes these loans are non-transparent even to the government of the borrowing country, if contracted by a SOE unbeknownst to the government.

Lack of public oversight of resource-backed finance agreements can push governments into debt distress, put sovereignty over public assets at risk, interrupt access to assistance from international financial institutions, and stifle the long-term development of borrowing countries.

2.2.5. Government-to-government sales

Governments may direct an SOE to sell commodities to another government for commercial or political reasons. The direct offer of commodities to other governments could be a method to secure long-term buyers for those commodities or may be in pursuit of unrelated foreign policy objectives. The use of this method has been documented in sales of commodities from Colombia, Nigeria, the Russian Federation and Venezuela.

In Colombia, in 2017, Ecopetrol sold 24.5% of the total value of its commodity sales via SOE to SOE arrangements. The 2018 *Invitation to Tender for the Sale and Purchase of Nigerian Crude Oil Grades* sets out a list of the types of buyers who may apply and includes "Government to Government arrangement (Bilateral relationships) with high energy consuming countries" (NNPC, 2018[16]).

Since the 1970s, NNPC has regularly sold crude oil to other countries, including BRICs, a few state-owned West African refiners, and other smaller African countries who do not always have refineries. These government-to-government sales are estimated to range from 8% to 24% of NNPC's total oil sales (Sayne, Gillies and Katsouris, 2015[14]).

2.3. Determining the allocation method for buyer selection

> **Box 2.2. What SOEs and governments can do to reduce opacity in the bidding process**
>
> - Make information related to all stages of bidding processes publicly available to all stakeholders. Such information may include timelines for submitting bids, selection and evaluation criteria, contract award decisions as well as other critical information, such as the list of applicants (OECD, 2014a);
>
> - Disclose any material deviations from the applicable legal and regulatory framework governing the selection of buying companies (Requirement 4.2(b), 2019 EITI Standard);
>
> - Appoint independent bodies responsible for the technical design of the bid and the oversight of the bidding process (ICAC, 2013);
>
> - Ensure effective management of possible conflicts of interest and clear segregation of roles (design, evaluation and selection of the bid);
>
> - Where possible, put in place an online submission process to increase transparency and limit interaction between SOE employees in charge of the bidding process and bidders;
>
> - Debrief bidders on how the award decision was made;
>
> - Establish dispute mechanisms to enable losing bidders to challenge the results in case of discontent; and
>
> - Mandate that awarded commodity sale agreements are fully disclosed in publicly available registries and open to scrutiny.
>
> *Source*: Adapted from (OECD, 2016[5]).

SOEs will need to decide which buyer selection method is most appropriate in each given context, and should develop a robust framework that sets out how this decision is made. SOEs may use a competitive bidding process, a direct negotiation with the buyer or a mix of both of these methods. Often the choice of the buyer selection method depends on the market for the particular commodity or other factors, such as when commodities are sold under resource-backed finance agreements.

For example, in Colombia, the particular buyer selection method is defined by the availability of crude oil at a given point in time and refined products as well as Ecopetrol's commercial strategy. Consequently, Ecopetrol sells approximately 85% of crude oil through a direct negotiation method and sells approximately 90% of refined products through a competitive bidding process (OECD Development Centre, 2018[9]).

SOEs should use a competitive bidding process, unless there are specific reasons for using a different method. In some situations, a competitive bidding process to select buyers may not be appropriate. These include instances where governments and/or SOEs are seeking loans from a buyer where repayment is made directly by the future production of natural resources (resource-backed financing agreement), or where SOEs wish to establish a long-term commercial relationship with an end user for commercial or strategic reasons (OECD Development Centre, 2018[17]). Prior to each buyer selection process, SOEs should disclose the buyer selection method that will be used and an explanation on why that particular procedure was selected.

2.3.1. Direct negotiation with buyer

This method involves the direct negotiation of a commodity sale agreement between the SOE and a buyer in a non-competitive context.

Factors that may lead to the decision to sell commodities by this method may include the desire for a long-term commercial relationship with an end user (e.g. refinery) or the perceived lack of interest by buyers which would not justify the cost and resourcing of a competitive bidding process.

SOEs that choose to sell commodities by directly negotiating with a buyer should ensure that the buyer can satisfy the minimum selection criteria and has the capability to give effect to its obligations under the commodity sale contract (see Section 2.4 below).

> **Box 2.3. What SOEs can do to reduce corruption risk in direct negotiations**
>
> - Disclose the reason(s) for why a direct negotiation was chosen over a competitive bidding process. This method of buyer selection does not necessarily justify less transparency. On the contrary, it may require even more transparency to mitigate risks of corruption;
>
> - Develop standardised models or guidelines for contractual terms in order to minimise discretion in direct negotiations;
>
> - Appoint an independent probity advisor (ideally from outside the SOE) who should be present at key points of the decision-making process and who should observe the negotiations with the buyer;
>
> - Conduct an independent review or audit following each use of the direct negotiation method; and
>
> - Require parliamentary approval for entering into significant long-term commodity sales agreements through direct negotiations.
>
> *Source:* Adapted from (OECD, 2009[18]).

2.3.2. Competitive selection

> **Box 2.4. What SOEs can do to reduce risks of bid rigging in a competitive selection process**
>
> **Be informed before designing the competitive selection process**
>
> - Be aware of the characteristics of the specific commodity market and trends that may affect competition for a competitive selection process;
> - Determine whether the specific commodity market has characteristics that make collusion more likely;
> - Be informed about pricing in neighbouring geographic areas for similar commodities, and collect information about past competitive selection processes for the same or similar commodities;
> - Ensure that if external consultants are used to help with estimate pricing that they have signed confidentiality agreements.
>
> **Design the competitive selection process to maximise the potential participation of genuinely competing bidders**
>
> - Consider reducing any constraints on the participation of foreign bidders in the competitive selection process;
> - Reduce the preparation costs – i.e. by using an electronic bidding system;
> - Do not unnecessarily limit the number of bidders in the bidding process.
>
> **Design the competitive selection process to effectively reduce communication among bidders**
>
> - Limit as much as possible communications between bidders during the competitive selection process. A requirement that bids must be submitted in person provides an opportunity for last minute communication between rival buyers. This could be prevented, for example, by using electronic bidding;
> - When disclosing information about a completed competitive selection process, avoid disclosing competitively sensitive information as this can facilitate the formation of bid-rigging schemes, going forward;
> - Include in the tender/auction offer a warning regarding the sanctions for bid rigging, e.g. suspension from participating in tenders/auctions for a certain period, the possibility for the SOE to seek damages, and any sanctions under the competition law.
>
> **Carefully determine the selection criteria**
>
> - When designing the selection process, think of the impact that the choice of criteria will have on future competition;
> - Whenever evaluating bidders on criteria other than price (e.g. technical aspects, local content requirements, etc.) such criteria need to be described and weighted adequately in advance in order to avoid post-award challenges;
> - Reserve the right not to award the contract if it is suspected that the bidding outcome is not competitive.
>
> *Source:* Adapted from (OECD, 2009[19]).

A competitive selection refers to the process where two or more potential buyers submit competitive bids that are assessed against set criteria, and where a commodity sale contract is awarded to the winning bidder. A competitive selection may be referred to as a tender, an auction, a bidding process/bidding round or other similar terms.

The majority of the SOEs surveyed by the OECD Development Centre in 2018 reported that a competitive bidding process was their preferred method of buyer selection. This applied equally across national oil companies and national mining companies.

A competitive selection process can be used to encourage the submission of several quality bids from established and legitimate buyers. However, SOEs should ensure that the competitive selection process is designed to promote competition and to reduce the risk of corruption or the manipulation of the process.

SOEs should be aware of the potential for bid rigging, i.e. agreements between bidders to eliminate competition in the selection process, which is a major risk to the effectiveness and integrity of the sale process and can deprive the SOE, and ultimately the state, of the genuine proceeds from the sales of its natural resources.

Bid rigging happens when potential buyers interfere with the standard operation of a competitive tender, for example, by conspiring to lower the price offered for the purchase of publicly owned commodities. Efficient and competitive selection processes are thus key to preventing this practice. Bid rigging is more likely to occur when a small number of companies participate in a competitive selection process. The fewer the number of buyers, the easier it is for them to reach an agreement on how to rig bids.

Prior to holding a competitive selection process, SOEs should determine an internal threshold of a minimum number of bidders where collusion or bid rigging would be highly unlikely. Subsequently, if a competitive selection process is held where the number of bidders falls below that threshold, this will signal that further scrutiny is required.

In addition, each competitive selection process should be audited and the audit should, among other things, seek to identify any instances where bid rigging/collusion may have occurred.

SOEs may choose to set a price threshold for a competitive selection process to protect the SOE from a situation where the highest bid is significantly below market value. For example, in Botswana, Okavango Diamond Company (ODC) may at any time before the commencement of an auction set a reserve price at which it is willing to sell each lot of diamonds. In this situation, ODC is not obliged to disclose this reserve price to any bidder (Okavango Diamond Company, 2019[20]).

> **Box 2.5. What SOEs can do to detect bid rigging in a competitive selection process**
>
> **Red flags when buyers are submitting bids**
>
> - Certain companies always submit bids but never win;
> - Each company seems to take a turn being the winning bidder;
> - Some companies unexpectedly withdraw from bidding;
> - There are an unusually low number of bids.
>
> **Red flags in the documents submitted with the bid**
>
> - Identical mistakes in the bid documents submitted by different companies, such as spelling errors;
> - Bids from different companies contain similar handwriting or typeface or use identical forms or stationery;
> - Bid documents from different companies indicate numerous last minute adjustments, such as the use of erasures or other physical alterations.
>
> **Red flags in the behaviour of the bidders**
>
> - A company submits both its own and a competitors bid;
> - A bid is submitted by a company that is incapable of successfully completing the contract;
> - Several bidders make similar enquiries to the SOE or submit similar requests or materials.
>
> *Source:* Adapted from (OECD, 2009[19]).

SOEs can make use of technology to design and carryout robust competitive selection processes. For example, in Botswana, ODC uses a transparent online platform to enable the sale of diamonds by auction.

ODC requires buyers to register in order to be qualified to participate in diamond auctions. The registration process is conducted entirely online, which improves efficiency but also limits the amount of human interface between the SOE and potential buyers prior to the actual buyer selection.

Once registered, potential buyers are able to participate in ODC's diamond auctions. These auctions take place online using a secure and fully auditable online auction system that was developed by a leading online auction provider. During the course of the auction, bidders are provided with real time auction feedback allowing them to make informed bidding decisions. The auction process cannot be manipulated by the company and the results are based on purely commercial considerations (highest bidder wins).

Within 24 hours of an auction taking place, the sales results and the prices paid are publicly available on the ODC website. The winning bid is disclosed and invoices are sent out within a 12 hour period. The use of a fully online auction platform can assist transparency and accountability. The ODC auction process is fully auditable as each click of the mouse by bidders (successful and unsuccessful) can be tracked and audited (OECD Development Centre, 2019[21]).

2.4. Setting out the terms of the buyer selection process

2.4.1. Pre-qualification process

The pre-qualification of potential buyers can provide a set of reliable buyers with an adequate standard of financial and technical capability, and can provide SOEs with more time to focus on the second part of the bid process, including the pricing/valuation of the commodity. In terms of the criteria used to select buyers, two main components are ordinarily set out:

- technical capability – the ability of the prospective buyers' to lift the commodity and their commercial experience with markets; and
- financial capability – the potential buyers' credit rating, bank credit line, etc.

In some jurisdictions, local participation may be an additional component if the state seeks to develop the local capacity for trading. For example, both GNPC (Ghana) and NNPC (Nigeria) have set out criteria for local content requirements.

The pre-qualification process can act a 'first check' of a company's credibility before a more thorough assessment is undertaken later, or can act as a screening process to ensure that only companies that fit a certain profile can move forward to the next stage.

SOEs should prevent the manipulation or abuse of the pre-qualification process, in particular by politically connected briefcase companies. Section 3.2 provides additional guidance on how SOEs can undertake due diligence on potential buyers.

SOEs should ensure that potential buyers are required to submit sufficient and detailed documentation to enable a robust assessment of their value proposition. For example, in Botswana, ODC undertakes a two-stage process to pre-qualify potential buyers.

Firstly, an internal audit is undertaken to assess whether there are any issues with the potential buyer that could bring ODC or Botswana into disrepute. This includes a background check on both the parent and subsidiaries of the potential buyer. If the potential buyer passes the first stage, an independent verification check is then undertaken. ODC will send the pre-qualification application to a third party agency that has access to relevant global databases to undertake a second check, which includes compliance with anti-money laundering (AML) requirements and international sanctions. ODC allows intermediaries to participate in the sales process but must go through the same two-stage screening process and satisfy the same requirements.

Once an SOE has screened a prospective buyer who satisfied the requirements, they are placed on a list of companies who may participate in future competitive bidding processes. SOEs should revisit this list of pre-qualified prospective buyers regularly to ensure that those companies continue to meet the criteria. For example, GNPC and Staatsolie perform this check before each tender/sale, Ecopetrol and Petrotrin perform this check annually (OECD Development Centre, 2018[9]). In Botswana, ODC reviews its pre-qualified buyers every three years to ensure ongoing compliance with globally accepted ethical trading. SOEs should consider disclosing the list of pre-qualified prospective buyers (see Box 3.1).

2.4.2. Pre-defined criteria to select buyers

Pre-defined criteria can be applied at different stages during the selection process. The assessment of a buyer against pre-defined criteria may occur at a pre-qualification stage, at a subsequent assessment stage (i.e. during a tender), or, as is often the case, during both stages.

An SOE will likely tailor its pre-defined criteria to the nature of the commodity being sold and other commercial and strategic factors but may also take into account domestic (political, economic and social) concerns. For example, in Mozambique, when selecting buyers of tranches of natural gas, ENH takes into account the quantity of the gas required and the price proposal but will also consider: employment, development of social infrastructure, local content and the involvement of public and private partnerships. In Mexico, PMI executes its oil marketing strategy by selecting buyers in the international market according to several factors, including: the type of crude oil, volume and term of availability, international market conditions (global and regional supply/demand, price, plant capacity, operation rates, outages) and quality, alongside the prospective buyer's financial and technical capabilities. As with NNPC in Nigeria, PMI also requires its buyers to fit a certain business model – they must be end users (i.e. refineries).

SOEs should ensure that their pre-defined criteria includes a requirement for the buyer to provide sufficient information to enable verification of the buyer and its beneficial owners.

Technical capability

SOEs should set out technical criteria that a prospective buyers must meet in order to ensure that the buyer is able to lift, process, refine, and/or use the commodity in question. For example, in Mexico, PMI assesses the type of crude oil, volume and term of availability, international market conditions and quality, alongside the prospective buyer's technical capabilities.

In Ghana, GNPC will send a request for proposal (RFP) to selected companies on GNPC's list of pre-qualified buyers based on the grade of the particular crude oil and the experience of the pre-qualified buyers. GNPC focuses on the prospective buyer's ability to lift a cargo of crude oil, as well as their commercial strategy. When selecting a marketer, GNPC will take into account the companies experience and flexibility in marketing crude oil, as well as health, safety and environment (HSE) capacity building factors.

SOEs can seek to optimise the value of their commodities by identifying the market where that commodity will yield the best value, and including this factor in their selection criteria. For example, it has been noted that for many NOCs, Asia has been the highest value market for crude oil in recent years (Van Schaik, 2012[13]).

In Iraq, SOMO takes into account the location of the prospective buyer by giving priority to the Asian market, while also considering giving priority to companies that hold large refining capacities, and promoting the expansion of Iraqi crude oil in key global markets. To this end, SOMO classify prospective buyers into three categories:

- Reputed International Oil Companies: well-known international oil companies (big and medium size), independent, governmental, well-structured companies that have refining capabilities and distribution network in many countries.

- Refining Companies: companies majoring in the refining industry and distribution of oil products.

- Authorised Companies: companies classified as main providers to refining companies in their country (IEITI, 2016[22]).

Financial capability

SOEs should set out financial criteria in order to gain an understanding of the prospective buyer's ability to make payment to the SOE for the commodities concerned. This may require prospective buyers to provide evidence of a line or credit from a reputable financial institution or to demonstrate their ability to directly pay for commodities they wish to purchase. SOEs should ensure that they have sufficient expertise and resources to conduct a thorough assessment of the financial information provided.

For example, in Colombia, Ecopetrol requires evidence of the buyer's financial capability and also carries out their own analysis of the buyer's liquidity, solvency, and profitability ratios and third-party rating reports. In Suriname, Staatsolie require prospective buyers to provide information on its company details, banking details and annual reports.

Box 2.6. Financial information required by NNPC at the pre-qualification stage

- Audited accounts for the past three years which must bear the stamp of the audit firm;

- A demonstration of minimum annual turnover of USD 500 million (or the Naira equivalent) and net worth of not less than USD 250 million (or the Naira equivalent) for the financial year ending of 2016; and

- The ability to establish an irrevocable letter of credit for the payment of any allocated crude oil subject to the contract terms – to ensure that the prospective buyer is able to pay for the shipment of crude oil is wishes to purchase.

Source: (NNPC, 2018[16]).

Local participation

SOEs may include local content requirements in their selection criteria in order to boost the participation of local entities in the commodities value chain. This requirement may be a specific policy set by the SOE or may be in accordance with a broader legislative requirements.

When SOEs set stringent criteria for the selection of buyers, this can result in local companies being outbid by large international buyers that are more able to meet these stringent criteria. Consequently, the inclusion of local content requirements in the buyer selection process can assist a country in developing its local trading capacity (OECD Development Centre, 2018[17]).

Local content requirements are ordinarily intended to encourage the participation of local entities as joint venture partners, rather than as the sole buyer in the transaction. SOEs should be aware that the requirement to involve a local joint venture partner in a sales transaction carries increased corruption risk, especially in cases where there is an absence of clear rules for the identification of the local company or where discretion is left to the government to identify such local partners (OECD, 2016[5]).

In order to reduce corruption risks associated with local participation, SOEs should set out clear, specific, objective criteria for the selection of a local partner in order to reduce discretion being applied on a case-by-case basis, and should ensure that all information related to existing local content requirements and pre-qualification criteria publicly available and easily accessible.

Where local content targets are in place, SOEs should also assess whether they reflect the sector's needs and available local capabilities. In terms of potential local partners, SOEs should establish a register based on certification schemes or objective and publicly available evaluation criteria, and ensure mechanisms for banning local enterprises from the register for a defined period of time in cases of non-compliance with anti-corruption laws and policies, and depending on the seriousness of the violation concerned (OECD, 2016[5]).

Box 2.7. What SOEs can do to reduce corruption risks associated with local participation

Identification of red flags:

- The local company and/or its principals have no prior relevant operational experience;

- The local company and/or its principals have little or no industry reputation or name recognition;

- The local company was incorporated or otherwise legally registered only shortly before, or even after, the commodity sale. It may appear that the local company was set up specifically for this particular commodity sales transaction.

Source: Adapted from (Sayne, Gillies and Watkins, 2017[23]).

Local content requirements are more prevalent in oil and gas sales than mineral sales. For example, in Nigeria, NNPC's *Invitation to Tender for the Sale and Purchase of Nigerian Crude Oil Grades* states that "compliance with Nigerian Content Act shall be a major consideration in the selection of applicants to lift Nigerian crude oil. It should be noted that evidence of Nigerian equity in the entity seeking consideration shall give competitive advantage" (NNPC, 2018[16]).

In Ghana, GNPC requires each buyer of its crude oil cargoes to have a "local partner", whist in Mozambique, ENH when selecting buyers of tranches of natural gas, takes into account local content, employment, and development of social infrastructure (OECD Development Centre, 2018[9]).

Additional criteria

In addition to the financial, technical and local content criteria set out above, SOEs may wish to include criteria to screen potential buyers' on their integrity. For example, this may include criteria in respect of: anti-corruption, ethics, as well as corporate social responsibility (CSR), including environmental, social, and labour standards.

SOEs may consider the inclusion of additional criteria in response to the many corruption challenges that can arise in commodity trading transactions.

SOEs will need to decide which specific criteria to include (anti-corruption, environmental etc.), and then potential buyers should be required to provide sufficient information on these aspects, including their corporate policies, to enable verification and assessment by the SOE.

Weighting of marks

In order to reduce the exercise of discretion in the buyer selection process, SOEs should use a weighting system to assess a prospective buyer against the pre-defined criteria.

A weighting system can assist in situations where a prospective buyer may be able to demonstrate its ability to meet some of the criteria but may have difficulty in meeting other criteria. A weighting system can also assist SOEs in determining the extent that non-financial and technical criteria, for example, local content requirements, should be taken into account.

SOEs that use a weighting system should clearly set out the parameters of this system in advance. For example, in Mozambique, ENH sets out its weighting system in the terms of reference for its natural gas tenders. ENH's weighting system takes into account five key factors when assessing a buyer against its buyer selection criteria (Mozambique Ministry of Energy and Mineral Resources, 2016[24]):

- Documents are in compliance with the law (20%)
- Social impact of the project (10%)
- Economic impact of the project (20%)
- Quantity of gas required (10%)
- Price proposal (30%).

Table 2.1. Weighting criteria used in the buyer selection process by GNPC

Technical terms (75%)	Ability to lift and strategy (15%)	Shipping	3%
		Experience in trading crudes	4%
		Refineries/options	3%
		Sales/marketing strategy	5%
	Flexibility of marketing (10%)	Ownership/access to dedicated vessels	2%
		Access to wider market	5%
	Experience in marketing new crude oil (10%)	Access/partnership with refineries	3%
		Number of crudes marketed	6%
		Marketing West African crudes	4%
	HSE (5%)	Proof of good safety record	5%
	Capacity building (5%)	Provision of training for GNPC staff	5%
	Local content (30%)	Evidence and terms of partnership	5%
		Strength of local partner	10%
		In-country presence & investment	15%
Commercial terms (25%)	Strategy to achieve the best price (differential) proposed		10%
	Marketing fee		5%
	Pricing option		5%

Note: This criteria may be tweaked by GNPC to suit particular situations – for example, the *Technical criteria – Experience in marketing new crude oil* – will be included for a tender of a new crude but not for an established crude.
Source: Adapted from the presentation by GNPC to the Tenth Plenary Meeting of the Policy Dialogue on Natural Resource-based Development on 26 June 2018.

2.5. Establishing a pricing policy

> **Box 2.8. What SOEs can do to prevent losses associated with commodity mispricing**
>
> - Set a clear pricing formula derived from publicly quoted prices prior to entering into negotiations with a buyer or holding a competitive selection process;
> - Utilise commodity benchmarks (with a premium or a discount adjustment to suit the specific commodity/circumstances) where applicable;
> - Consider disclosing pricing formula to market participants; and
> - Include a pricing adjustment mechanism in long-term sales agreements to ensure that prices are reviewed in order to reflect market value across the life of the contract.

2.5.1. Overview

Undervaluation and mispricing can result in significant revenue losses for an SOE. Mispricing in commodity trading usually consists of under-reporting volumes or under-invoicing the value of the resource sold, allowing its purchaser to resell it at an inflated margin.

Pricing may be affected by the choice of contract (spot sales, term arrangement) that underlies the commodity sale transaction. For example, a buyer entering into a commercial relationship with the seller to purchase a commodity over a long time horizon, and therefore providing a reasonable certainty of future revenue for the SOE, may have this factor reflected in the sale price.

Consequently, SOEs should ensure that a robust pricing policy/formula derived from publicly quoted prices that reflect market value is developed prior to entering into negotiations with a buyer or holding a competitive bidding process.

For example, in Ghana, GNPC uses the following pricing formula when selecting buyers for crude oil cargoes: Unit price (USD/Bbl.) = Dated Brent Price + Differential + Pricing Option Fee minus Marketing Fees (if Applicable). For example, in GNPCs offtake agreements, the buyer has a choice of four different pricing options. Any option exercised by the buyer attracts a margin. The options are:

- The average of five consecutive Platts Crude Oil Marketwire of the mean of Dated Brent quotations published around the Bill of Lading date (BL Date) – i.e. the two quotations before the BL date; the BL date quotation and the two days quotations following the BL date;
- The average of five consecutive Plates Crude Oil Marketwire of the mean of Dated Brent quotations published immediately prior to the BL date;
- The average of five consecutive Plates Crude Oil Marketwire of the mean of Dated Brent quotations published immediately after the BL date;
- The monthly average of Platts Crude Oil Marketwire Dated Brent price quotations for the BL Month of Lifting (GHEITI, 2018[12]).

> **Box 2.9. Pricing policy for the sale of crude oil by NNPC**
>
> NNPC sets sale prices for each of Nigeria's 26 grades of crude oil on a monthly basis. Specifically, most of the oil NNPC sells for export is valued using a widely-used formula pricing system called "official selling prices" (OSPs). Each OSP has three components:
>
> - Benchmark. This is an average of five consecutive price quotations for Brent crude, as published by the trade periodical Platts;
> - Differential. This is the premium or discount to Brent, expressed in dollars per barrel, that is supposed to reflect the market value of the particular crude grade vis-à-vis Brent. NNPC publishes a new differential once per month for each of the country's 26 crude grades;
> - Pricing Option. This feature allows a buyer to pay a small premium – usually USD 0.05 to USD 0.10 per barrel – which entitles the buyer to choose before lifting which five-day Brent quotations NNPC will use to price the cargo.
>
> *Source:* (Sayne, Gillies and Katsouris, 2015[14]).

2.5.2. Use of a commodity benchmark

Transactions that take place in the market are often reported by specialised agencies (such as Platts or Argus) and are used as a basis for the determination of the benchmarks for different commodities, particularly crude oil grades. SOEs may need to determine for themselves an official selling price (OSP) for their commodity as a premium or a discount against the relevant benchmark. This determination will take into account several factors, including quality and location.

SOEs should ensure that their pricing formulas are market based and derived from publicly quoted commodity prices where available.

SOEs should be aware that corruption risks may be heightened for commodity sales where there is a lack of publicly quoted prices for the commodity, as is the case with some minerals. Many governments have concerns around their ability to value these commodities and may be losing revenue as a result.

The challenge that many SOEs are facing is linked to the fact that they usually do not sell finished products for which commercial prices are available, but they sell the raw ore or intermediate products for which reference prices are more difficult to establish. The OECD Centre for Tax and Policy Administration and the International Institute for Sustainable Development have jointly developed a practice note – *Monitoring the Value of Mineral Exports: Policy Options for Governments* – that sets out a framework for mineral valuation applicable to all minerals (IISD/OECD, 2018[25]). The recommended starting point is the commercial valuation of the mineral or metal, followed by downward adjustments for undesirable physical properties in the ore and upward adjustments for desirable physical properties or other valuable by-products. Optional steps relate to additional adjustments that might be made to account for specific economic circumstances (OECD Development Centre, 2019[26]).

Where there is a lack of publicly quoted prices for the commodity (e.g. lithium) SOEs can seek information from tax authorities collected from tax paying oil/mineral companies through documentation required by law or through audit activities undertaken by the tax administration. This approach requires strong information gathering power within tax administrations and the ability for tax administrations and SOEs to share information.

Although benchmarks for different commodities are more common for crude oil, institutions such as the London Metal Exchange publish daily prices for many minerals. For example, in Chile, Codelco's selling prices are based on the London Metal Exchange daily pricing, Metal Bulletin publication and London bullion prices.

Similarly, in the Democratic Republic of the Congo, Gécamines takes into account average prices set by the London Metal Exchange and the London Bullion Market with discounts relating to quality of the commodity as well as the transportation costs in respect of the valuation of its sales of cobalt, copper and zinc (RCS Global, 2018[27]).

2.5.3. Transparency of pricing information

Pricing and the process that SOEs use to determine prices are the issue of greatest interest and concern to many third-party users of the data. Consequently, introducing transparency in respect of pricing information can be an important tool through which SOEs can reduce opportunities for corruption and public rent diversion and guard against undervaluation and mispricing.

The EITI has outlined options that SOEs may wish to consider to increase transparency around pricing information:

- SOEs may provide a full explanation of how they generally determine their selling prices;
- SOEs may provide information about how they set monthly prices;
- SOEs may provide information about how the prices of individual sales are then determined (EITI, 2017[4]).

Several SOEs disclose their pricing formulas to market participants prior to entering into negotiating with a buyer or holding a competitive selection process.

For example, in Iraq, SOMO determines its OSP based on international markets but with adjustments made in respect of a premium or a discount from the previous month's advertised prices. The use of this OSP has brought an increased level of transparency to the buyer selection process in Iraq (IEITI, 2016[22]).

In Mexico, PMI sets out pricing formulas for each specific grade of Mexican crude oil to be placed at a specific market region within a determined pricing period agreed between PMI and buyer. Pricing formulas are based on international crude oil market quotes published by renowned international providers of energy and commodities information.

2.5.4. Pricing adjustment mechanism in long-term sales agreements

Many SOEs sell oil, gas and minerals under long-term sale arrangements, and in some cases, these agreements can exceed ten years duration. If sales prices are locked in for a significant period of time and commodity prices rise, SOEs can miss out on capturing the value from those price rises. Consequently, SOEs should include contractual mechanisms in their commodity sales agreements that provide for prices to be reviewed on a regular basis in order to reflect market value.

For example, in Mozambique, ENH enters into long-term gas sale arrangements for periods that usually exceed ten years. The gas price is adjusted using a specific price mechanism and indexations according to movements of the international market.

In Ghana, the length of some crude oil sales arrangements exceed ten years. Consequently, a provision is included in these agreements to adjust the differential based on daily published Platt's price quotations which are assessed daily, and so to ensure that these long-terms sales arrangements seek to reflect market value throughout the life of the contract.

2.6. Drafting the contractual provisions

> **Box 2.10. What SOEs can do to reduce risks associated with unbalanced contractual provisions**
>
> - Develop standardised model sale agreements in order to minimise discretion in contract negotiation;
> - Take the lead on drafting bespoke agreements rather than rely on agreements drafted by the buyer;
> - Include pre-defined commercial terms in sales agreements to simplify the buyer selection process and to reduce opportunities for discretion; and
> - Include a pricing adjustment mechanism in long-term sales agreements to ensure that prices are reviewed in order to reflect market value across the life of the contract.
>
> *Source:* Adapted from (OECD, 2016[5]).

The inclusion of unbalanced contractual provisions in commodity trading transactions can result in significant revenue losses for an SOE. Opaque or unclear contractual provisions can cause confusion and also may unduly favour the buyer.

Asymmetries of information between the SOE and the buyer as well as the lack of general transparency in commodity sale transactions constitute major risk factors for corruption.

Red flags that may indicate unbalanced contractual provisions include: unusual long-term repayment periods and payments in open credit where there is no financial guarantee (i.e. where the SOE assumes substantial risks of default). If these risks are identified, further scrutiny is recommended for this particular commodity sale transaction.

SOEs should develop model sales contracts or templates for use in all commodity transactions with buyers. These model contracts should be developed in advance of entering into negotiations with a buyer or holding a competitive selection process. Standardised model contracts can also reduce discretion in commodity transactions as many aspects of the contract will not be subject to negotiations.

If a model contact is not appropriate in a specific commodity sales context and a bespoke agreement is required, the SOE should take the lead in drafting that agreement rather than the buyer.

In order to simplify the buyer selection process and to reduce the opportunities for discretion, SOEs can include pre-defined commercial terms in their sales agreements.

The use of specific Incoterms in contractual provisions can also have an effect on the balance of the contract as they determine which party assumes which costs and which risks. Incoterms are pre-defined commercial terms published by the International Chamber of Commerce (ICC) that are commonly used in both international and domestic trade contracts.

Incoterms inform sales contracts defining respective obligations, costs, and risks involved in the delivery of goods from the seller to the buyer. The inclusion of Incoterms in a contract allows for the allocation of costs, risks and the transfer of title between the seller and the buyer. These can include loading, export clearance, fees, insurance, unloading and transportation cost from the arrival port to destination.

Several SOEs surveyed by the OECD Development Centre in 2018 reported the use of such pre-defined commercial terms. In respect of SOEs selling crude oil, the most commonly used Incoterms 2010 is Free-On-Board (FOB).

3. Carrying out the buyer selection process

3.1. Proactive transparency measures

> **Box 3.1. What SOEs can do to increase transparency and accountability in their commodity sales transactions**
>
> - Disclose the sales policy (guideline, directive etc.) and provide a description of the process for selecting the buying companies, e.g. a tender for a specific cargo, or the selection of term contract recipients;
>
> - Disclose the buyer selection criteria (technical, financial etc.) – in advance of a competitive tender or the beginning of a direct negotiation process;
>
> - Consider providing and explaining any special exemption and/or other deviation from the applicable legal and regulatory framework;
>
> - Disclose the list of pre-qualified buyers (where relevant) including beneficial ownership information;
>
> - Disclose the commodity sales contract or its key terms – price, volume, grade/quality, contract type (spot, term etc.) and duration. Where standardised contracts or general terms and conditions are used, SOEs should disclose the full text of the standard contract along with the text of any agreements that allow deviations from that standard;
>
> - Disclose the identity of the buyer; and
>
> - Disclose information in respect of the buyers' beneficial ownership.
>
> *Source:* Adapted from (EITI, 2017[4]).

Introducing transparency into the buyer selection process can be an important tool through which SOEs can reduce opportunities for corruption and public rent diversion and promote better public accountability of their operations.

SOEs may refer to requirement 4.2.b of the 2019 EITI Standard which provides that:

> *Implementing countries including state-owned enterprises are encouraged to disclose a description of the process for selecting the buying companies, the technical and financial criteria used to make the selection, the list of selected buying companies, any material deviations from the applicable legal and regulatory framework governing the selection of buying companies, and the related sales agreements (EITI, 2019[3]).*

SOEs can take steps to proactively disclose information before, during, and after a specific buyer selection process, whilst taking care to protect information of a commercially sensitive nature. SOEs should be transparent about what information will be disclosed and when those disclosures will take place in order for potential buyers to plan accordingly.

A decision to disclose information may be made by the SOE or may be set out in legislation. SOEs should be transparent with potential buyers from the beginning of the process about the scope of future disclosures. For example, SOEs may include provisions in their general terms and conditions to facilitate disclosures and to avoid legal issues being raised by buyers at the time of disclosure. SOEs may wish to consult with buyers prior to disclosure where appropriate, however, a buyer should not have a veto right over the disclosure of any information related to the sale of publicly-owned commodities should it be in the public interest to disclose that information.

3.1.1. Transparency of the SOE's sales policy

Providing greater transparency around the sales policy is one way that SOEs can reduce the opacity of their commodity trading transactions and the accompanying corruption risks. The majority of the SOEs surveyed by the OECD Development Centre in 2018 reported the existence of a specific policy (directive, guideline etc.) for sales of oil, gas and minerals, although that policy was not always disclosed (OECD Development Centre, 2018[9]).

Two examples of SOEs that do make their sales policies publicly available were identified in Mexico and Mozambique. In Mexico, PMI makes its *"Políticas comerciales de petróleo crudo"* available on its website. In Mozambique, the publicly available "Gas Master Plan" contains the sales policy for the tranches of natural gas that are the responsibility of ENH.

SOEs can take steps to clarify expectations from potential buyers by clearly setting out transparency provisions in their sales policies that enable the disclosure of key information in respect of the buyer selection process and future commodity sales transactions.

Box 3.2. Sales policy for the sale of crude oil by PMI

- PMI will seek, through the commercialization of crude oil, to maximize the value of PEMEX and of exports Mexican oil companies.

- PMI will seek to sell the crude oil that it exports to those final consumers that due to their particular characteristics (geographic location, configuration of their process equipment and others) derive greater value when processing crude oil Mexican and trying to establish a lasting business relationship.

- Mexican crude oil will be sold at a price composed of formulas that use the similar raw materials in the region or market where the Mexican crude oil is going to be processed, either United States of America (USA), countries of the rest of America, Europe (Northwest or Mediterranean) or Far East.

- Following the price guidelines established in this policy, PMI will offer the crude oil that it exports using the same price formula for all customers that are located in a predetermined geographic region. PMI may place shipments in conditions other than those referred to in these Commercial Policies in cases of force majeure, situations particular logistics or inventories of Pemex Exploration and Production, test shipments, raw with qualities different from the typical exports or when the Board of Directors of the Company approves it.

- PMI will seek the establishment of stable and lasting business relationships only with final consumers (including strategic reserves of countries with which Mexico has diplomatic relations). Notwithstanding the foregoing, PMI will be able to sell crude oil to the company PMI Trading, Ltd, for warehouse purposes and mixed to

> capture market opportunities that result in an economic benefit for the PEMEX group, but the subsequent sale of the crude must be done to final consumers.
>
> - PMI will endeavour to ensure that any sale of Mexican crude oil is carried out with a ban on resale, unless it has express authorization. It will not be considered resale, when a customer for operational or logistical reasons related to the used or the situation of your refinery request to exchange one or more shipments of crude oil with another client, situation that must be previously approved by PMI.
>
> - Trying to mitigate the credit risk, when any of the clients of crude oil does not have the financial solidity for PMI to authorize open credit and cannot grant the bank guarantees established in the Credit Manual of PMI, the Company may accept that the payment of crude oil sold to the customer is made by a third party with the understanding that the crude oil sold will be refined in the facilities of the original customer with whom the commercial relationship will be maintained. The third party that makes payments to PMI must be approved in accordance with the provisions of the Credit Manual. The sales under this scheme, they will not be considered as being carried out through an intermediary in accordance with the provisions of Article 5.1.5 of these Commercial Policies.
>
> *Source:* (P.M.I.® Comercio Internacional, S.A. de C.V., 2018[28]).

3.1.2. Disclosure of the buyer selection criteria

SOEs can introduce greater transparency into the buyer selection process by publicly disclosing their buyer selection criteria in advance of a competitive tender or the beginning of a direct negotiation process. This practice is encouraged by the Requirement 4.2.b of the 2019 EITI Standard, which provides that "implementing countries including state-owned enterprises are encouraged to disclose a description of the process for selecting the buying companies, the technical and financial criteria used to make the selection" (EITI, 2019[3]).

This advance disclosure of buyer selection criteria can assist buyers in submitting higher quality bids that aim to meet the requirements that the SOE has previously set out. This can act to improve the overall efficiency of the buyer selection process as the buyer selection team should have a complete bid/application to assess and this should also minimise the interaction between the buyer selection team and the prospective buyers during the selection process – which itself can create avenues for corruption.

Several SOEs routinely disclose their buyer selection criteria. In Mexico, PMI sets out and discloses criteria for prospective buyers to determine whether they are able to enter into sales contracts with PMI. This criteria includes whether buyers are based in countries with which the Mexican government allows commercial relations, whether they are final consumers of crude oil, their financial situation and ability to pay, and their obligation not to on-sell the crude to other buyers. Other examples of the proactive disclosure of buyer selection criteria can be seen in Mozambique (ENH) and Myanmar (Myanmar Gems Enterprise). In Ghana, GNPC does not disclose its buyer selection criteria publicly but will provide a copy of its criteria to potential bidders on request.

In terms of the scope of the disclosure of the buyer selection criteria, SOEs should at a minimum, disclose: a description of the process for selecting the buying companies, e.g. a tender for a specific cargo, or the selection of term contract recipients; the selection criteria itself (technical, financial, local content requirements etc.); information on any special exemption and/or other deviation from the applicable legal and regulatory framework (EITI, 2017[4]).

3.1.3. Disclosure of the commodity sales contract or its key terms

There is an increasing international trend towards extractive contract transparency where SOEs can take proactive steps to reduce the opacity that often surrounds commodity trading transactions. The EITI has documented how enhanced transparency in commodity trading supports greater competition and can result in reputational gains for the actors in commodity sales transactions (EITI, 2019[29]).

Requirement 4.2.b of the 2019 EITI Standard provides that "implementing countries including state-owned enterprises are encouraged to disclose ... the list of selected buying companies ... and the related sales agreements" (EITI, 2019[3]).

The EITI recommends that SOEs should consider the disclosure of the commodity sales contract (EITI, 2019[3]). Where disclosure of the contract in its entirety is not feasible, SOEs should disclose the key terms of the sales contract, including (but not limited to): price, volume, grade/quality, contract type (spot, term etc.) and duration.

Several SOEs have begun disclosing limited details of the terms of their sales contracts. In Mozambique, ENH discloses the quantity of gas allocated to each project/buyer but does not disclose the price and other commercial terms. In Zimbabwe, MMCZ provides certain information in respect to the quantity, quality and term length of the sales contracts. This information is not released immediately but is available after the end of a financial year and only after it has been audited (OECD Development Centre, 2018[9]).

3.1.4. Disclosure of the identity of buyers

It is important for the identity of the buyer to be fully transparent to ensure that the SOE is entering into an arrangement with an entity that is known, and that has the requisite financial and technical capacity to meet its obligations under the contract. Consequently, SOEs should publicly disclose the identity of the buyer for each commodity sales transaction.

In order to provide meaningful information in respect of the identity of the buyer, SOEs should provide the full name and country of registration of the buying company, company registration number, and the name of the parent company (if applicable).

Several of the SOEs surveyed by the OECD Development Centre in 2018 disclose the identity of the buyer. These include: Albpetrol, ENH, MMCZ, Nilepet and NNPC (who publish a crude oil off-takers list on their website). Albpetrol and ENH go one-step further and also publish the identity of unsuccessful bidders in order to provide greater transparency to their operations (OECD Development Centre, 2018[9]).

3.1.5. Disclosure of the buyers' beneficial ownership information

The beneficial owner(s) of the buyer refers to the natural person(s) who directly or indirectly ultimately own or control the buyer. This is distinct from the 'legal owners' who are the persons or companies listed as direct owners in a company's corporate registration, tax returns, licences or contracts.

In the extractives sector, there is evidence that hidden ownership information is a risk factor for corruption. The NRGI reviewed 100 oil, gas and mining corruption cases from

49 countries, and found that over half of these cases involved companies with hidden beneficial owners (Sayne, Gillies and Watkins, 2017[23]).

There had been increasing global awareness of the importance of beneficial ownership information disclosure. The existing global norm on ensuring availability of beneficial ownership information for corporate vehicles is contained in the FATF Recommendations 2012 – Recommendations 24 and 25 and Immediate Outcome 5. This definition of beneficial ownership was adopted by the OECD-hosted Global Forum on Transparency and Exchange of Information for Tax Purposes in 2016, and represents the most widely established international standard for ensuring the availability of beneficial ownership information.

Both the EITI and the European Union have set deadlines for beneficial ownership transparency. EITI implementing countries were required to introduce public beneficial ownership for companies bidding for licences or holding a licence to explore or exploit oil, gas or minerals by 1 January 2020. These EITI requirements have sparked reform in 20 countries now working on establishing public registers. The *EU Fifth Anti-Money Laundering Directive*, which entered into force in July 2018, required EU member states to incorporate beneficial ownership transparency into domestic legislation by January 2020.

SOEs should ensure that they have access to buyers' beneficial ownership information. For example, SOEs could collect this information from the buyer as part of a competitive tender process or when entering into direct negotiations. This information should then be stored for future use. For example, the EITI recommends that SOEs maintain an up-to-date list of approved buying companies and include beneficial ownership information for each approved buyer (EITI, 2017[4]).

In terms of the information to be collected, the EITI recommends that information about the identity of the beneficial owner should include the name of the beneficial owner, the nationality, and the country of residence, as well as identifying any politically exposed persons (EITI, 2019[3]).

SOEs should disclose the buyers' beneficial ownership information to increase transparency in the buyer selection process, and to assure citizens of the bona fide nature of the buyers of publicly-owned commodities. The EITI further recommends that SOEs should consider disclosing the list of approved buying companies and their beneficial ownership information (EITI, 2017[4]).

3.2. Undertaking due diligence on buyers

Box 3.3. What SOEs can do to undertake effective due diligence on buyers

- Determine what information should be requested from potential buyers in advance of a competitive tender or the beginning of a direct negotiation process;

- At a minimum, include information on the beneficial ownership of the buyer, the involvement of any politically-exposed-persons, and the existence of any conflicts of interest;

- Verify that information and consider whether additional due diligence actions may be required in each commodity sale transaction; and

---

> - Identify any red flags, such as excessive complexity in a corporate vehicle structure or the involvement of a PEP.

SOEs should undertake robust screening of potential buyers prior to (see pre-qualification criteria Section 2.4.1) and during the buyer selection process, in order to gain a complete understanding of the buyer and its value proposition, and to identify any red flags.

SOEs should consider, in advance of a competitive tender or at the beginning of a direct negotiation process, what information should be requested from potential buyers, in order for the SOE to carry out effective due diligence. The information that SOEs may wish to request is broad but as a minimum should include information on, the beneficial ownership of the buyer, any involvement of politically exposed persons, and the existence of any conflicts of interest.

For example, in Nigeria, NNPCs invitation to tender for the purchase of crude oil specifies that all bidders must provide a written statement providing the full names, contact addresses of current directors and beneficial owners. In Mexico, PMI requires all prospective buyers to provide details of the main shareholders, their names and percentage interests, as well as the name and position of senior executives.

> **Box 3.4. Information required from buyers prior to entering into negotiations to purchase crude oil from Petrotrin**
>
> Prior to entering into any commercial arrangement, the following information must be submitted for review by Petrotrin:
>
> - Full name and registered address of the Supplier, including the following: a) Certification of the entity Registration. b) Declaration of the particulars of its Shareholders – name, occupation and address. c) Declaration of the Directors and key management personnel -name, occupation and address.
> - Description of type of business the company is engaged in and its experience in crude supply and trading (Company Profile).
> - Bank and business references with whom the company currently conducts business.
> - List of key management personnel.
> - Recent audited financial statements (3 years).
> - A list of references including financial institutions and commercial companies with whom the company currently conducts business.
> - Any rating that your company may have from institutions such as S&P and Moody's etc.
> - A Dunn and Bradstreet (D&B) report of the prospective buyer.
>
> *Source:* (OECD Development Centre, 2018[9]).

Once the requested information has been provided, SOEs should undertake an analysis of that information to check its accuracy and reliability, and consider whether steps need to be taken to verify that information and whether any additional due diligence is required.

At a minimum SOEs should identify and verify the beneficial owners of all relevant persons or entities, identify whether any beneficial owners are PEPs, conduct a background check to ascertain any materially relevant criminal, civil, or regulatory violations, and conduct a conflict-of-interest check on relevant natural persons (Votava, Hauch and Clementucci, 2018[30]).

For example, in Chile, Codelco performs market intelligence, media screening, reviews annual reports, and visits plants and offices of the prospective buyer. In Mexico, PMI undertake due diligence on prospective buyer's refineries, including verification of the ownership, configuration and capacity.

SOEs need to ensure that they are properly resourced to carry out checks and verification of potential buyers. This may include the provision of training for relevant SOE employees, having access to international databases, and establishing channels of communication with officials in other countries.

3.2.1. Beneficial ownership and involvement of politically exposed persons

---

Box 3.5. FATF Definition of politically exposed persons

Foreign PEPs are individuals who are or have been entrusted with prominent public functions by a foreign country, for example Heads of State or of government, senior politicians, senior government, judicial or military officials, senior executives of state owned corporations, important political party officials.

Domestic PEPs are individuals who are or have been entrusted domestically with prominent public functions, for example Heads of State or of government, senior politicians, senior government, judicial or military officials, senior executives of state owned corporations, important political party officials.

Persons who are or have been entrusted with a prominent function by an international organisation refers to members of senior management, i.e. directors, deputy directors and members of the board or equivalent functions.

The definition of PEPs is not intended to cover middle ranking or more junior individuals in the foregoing categories.

Source: (FATF, 2013[31]).

It is important for SOEs to fully understand the identity of the buyer's beneficial owners to reduce opportunities for corruption and public rent diversion, and to create greater accountability and public trust by ensuring that value is not lost in the transactions.

Corporate vehicles can be used to introduce opacity into the ownership structure of an entity to facilitate corruption schemes. They can provide "legal distance" between the beneficial owner and his/her assets by introducing complexity and obscure true ownership. SOEs should note that excessive complexity in a corporate vehicle structure can be regarded as a "red flag" indicator of risk, and may be intended to hide the identity of the beneficial owner.

In some cases the beneficial owner may be a politically exposed person (PEP) who may use corporate vehicles to obscure their identity in order to distance themselves from specific transactions. The risk of a PEPs involvement may be heightened in situations where contracts are awarded to local companies – either awarded outright or in a partnership between a local and an international buyer.

It is important to note that the PEP status itself does not necessarily mean an individual is corrupt or that they have been involved in any corrupt practice – but it does raise a red flag and SOEs should then apply further scrutiny.

SOEs should require potential buyers to submit anticorruption certifications, as well as beneficial ownership and PEP information as part of their bid or at the beginning of a direct negotiation procedure. This information should accurately describe how the beneficial owner holds his/her interest, and include a diagram or corporate organogram that visually shows the relationship, as well as the full corporate structure of the company (Westenberg and Sayne, 2018[32]).

In order to verify the beneficial ownership and PEP declarations provided by prospective buyers, SOEs should screen for obvious deficiencies in a bid that raise clear corruption risks, and should cross-reference the beneficial ownership information received from the buyer with information contained in centralised national or international beneficial ownership registers (Westenberg and Sayne, 2018[32]).

SOEs should also undertake their own open source verification of potential buyers by searching: copies of share registries, periodic regulatory filing reports (tax filings, public financial reports and required filings with securities regulator or other regulators), certificate of incorporation and other corporate formation documents, and documents that provide persons with authority to act on behalf of the corporation and define the scope of that authority (Votava, Hauch and Clementucci, 2018[30]).

SOEs may then undertake additional anti-corruption due diligence on potential buyers, prior to, or during, the buyer selection process. For example, in Chile, Codelco performs market intelligence, media screening, the review of annual reports, and visits to plants and offices of the prospective buyer. In Mexico, PMI undertake due diligence on prospective buyer's refineries, including verification of the ownership (OECD Development Centre, 2018[9]).

> **Box 3.6. Red flags that may indicate corruption risks associated with BOs and involvement of PEPs**
>
> - The company's beneficial ownership or PEP disclosures are uncertified or never submitted;
> - The company claims it has no beneficial owner, or that its beneficial owner cannot be identified;
> - The company identifies another company as its beneficial owner;
> - Cross-checks of the company's certifications and disclosures against the supporting documents provided reveal that one or more claims in the application is contradicted by the company's supporting documentation or other reliable information readily available to the SOE;
> - The disclosures in the application, or the SOEs verification efforts, shows that the company has a PEP as a beneficial owner that violates provisions in domestic anti-corruption law that prohibit public officials acquiring personal benefit from commodity sales; and

> - The disclosure strongly suggests the company has engaged in collusive or anti-competitive behaviour—e.g., multiple companies with the same beneficial owner bid for the same contract.
>
> *Source:* Adapted from (Westenberg and Sayne, 2018[32]).

3.2.2. Conflicts of interest

> **Box 3.7. OECD Definition of conflict of interest**
>
> A "conflict of interest" involves a conflict between the public duty and private interests of a public official, in which the public official has private-capacity interests which could improperly influence the performance of their official duties and responsibilities.
>
> *Source:* (OECD, 2003[10]).

SOEs should be cognisant of conflicts of interest that may exist between their employees and agents, and representatives of buyers. When conflict of interest situations are not properly identified, disclosed and managed, they can endanger the integrity of the SOE and can result in corruption and public rent diversion in a commodity sale transaction.

SOEs should require buyers to disclose any conflict of interest but should also undertake their own analysis to identify and capture any additional red flags associated with the relationship between the buyer and the seller. This may include whether any employees of the buyer are former employees of the SOE (or vice versa), whether the buyer has access to any information in respect of the commodity sale that other rival companies did not, or where the buyer is providing goods or services to the SOE (or government) that are unrelated to the commodity sale transaction.

SOEs should be particularly cognisant of the movement of personnel between SOEs and buyers (often termed 'revolving doors').

While a conflict of interest is not necessarily evidence of corruption itself, there is increasing recognition that conflicts between the private interests and public duties of public officials (which includes SOE employees), if inadequately managed, can result in corruption. Conflicts of interest cannot simply be avoided or prohibited, and must be identified, disclosed, and managed.

An example of a requirement for a buyer to declare certain conflicts of interest can be found in Nigeria, where, a company submitting a bid in a competitive tender for the purchase of crude oil from NNPC must provide a sworn affidavit to "confirm whether or not any of the members of relevant companies of NNPC or Bureau of Public Procurement (BPP) is former or present Director, Shareholder, or has any pecuniary interest in your company" (NNPC, 2018[16]).

3.2.3. Additional due diligence requirements

SOEs may need to undertake additional due diligence checks where necessary. This requirement may be triggered by the nature of the commodity that is being sold or by the identity of the buyer.

For example, in Zimbabwe, the Zimbabwe Consolidated Diamond Company (ZCDC) may subject buyers to an Interpol check and may require buyer to provide further information. In Colombia, if a buyer is classified as comprising high reputational risk, Ecopetrol may require:

- Visits or interviews to the counterparty;
- High levels of authority to approve the registration of the counterparty;
- Requirement of declarations and disclaimers for the specifics conditions (Ex, reported by restrictive lists);
- Monitoring the commercial activity with Ecopetrol S.A;
- Filling out the anti-corruption certificate that is part of the internal guidelines of Ecopetrol S.A. (OECD Development Centre, 2018[9]).

3.3. Countering public rent diversion at point of revenue collection

> **Box 3.8. What SOEs and governments can do to counter public rent diversion**
>
> - Favour clarity, simplicity and centralisation of the revenue collection process in agencies with appropriate revenue collection expertise and mandate to raise revenue;
> - Put in place an internal control system for revenue administration based on robust risk management and adequate human, financial and technical resources;
> - Consider designating an alternative entity to the SOE to receive the payment;
> - Provide credible avenues for whistleblowing against corrupt practices for officials, either within or outside the SOE.
>
> *Source:* Adapted from (OECD, 2016[5]).

SOEs and governments should be cognisant of the corruption risks associated with revenue collection where funds may be misappropriated or diverted for private gain.

These corruption risks can include the misreporting practices, mainly consisting of distortions in accounting and reporting of revenues. For example, the underreporting of production volumes and the misreporting of applicable charges, fees or credits. Diverted revenues are then usually transferred to bank accounts located in offshore jurisdictions with low tax liabilities and insufficient legislation on information disclosure on beneficial ownership.

SOEs and governments should consider implementing a payment model where the entity that receives the payment is different from the SOE that arranges the commodity sale. In this model, payment for the commodities would be made to a government account – for example the ministry of finance, treasury or central bank. Standard rules of public financial management would then apply.

For example, in Ghana, the Petroleum Revenue Management Act 2011 sets out a process where payments for crude oil sold by GNPC are paid by buyers directly into a specified account at the Bank of Ghana (central bank).

In Iraq, in the aftermath of the Oil-for-Food Programme scandal and the 2003 Iraq War, in an attempt to prevent oil sales from corruption risks or rent diversion, Iraqi authorities required that the payment of commodity sales proceeds must be directed to a different account from the one of the SOE SOMO (OECD Development Centre, 2018[17]).

Annex

Checklist: Questions that SOEs may consider during the buyer screening process

- What is the corruption profile and local business climate of the country in which the buyer is registered?

- Does the buyer rely on the use of agents or other intermediaries or third parties? If so, what is known of their integrity profiles?

- Do you have a clear indication of the ultimate beneficial owner(s) of the buyer?

- Is there a presence of politically-exposed persons (PEPs)? If so, why and are there any indications of conflicts of interest or misuse of position? Are you comfortable with their sources of wealth?

- What is the reputation of the buyer, including perceptions of its business conduct?

- What is the ownership structure of the buyer? For example, shell companies and companies registered in jurisdictions with strong secrecy laws may pose additional risks.

- Has the buyer been implicated in any instances of corruption (allegations, arrests, indictments) or been blacklisted by a government agency (in any jurisdiction)?

- Is the buyer listed on the debarment lists of international financial institutions?

- Has the buyer been involved in any litigation, whether civil, criminal or regulatory?

- Are any gifts or entertainment being offered?

- Are any political or charitable contributions being requested?

- What is the nature of any relationships the buyer may have with public officials?

- Have SOEs in other jurisdictions terminated their relationship with the buyer or banned the buyer from future commodity sales? If so, what were the reasons?

- Does the buyer have internal controls in place to prevent corruption in its business dealings?

- Does the buyer fully understand any relevant anti-corruption policy (set out in national legislation or SOEs anti-corruption guidelines)?

Source: Adapted from (OECD/AfDB, 2016[33]).

References

Deloitte (2018), *Extractive Industries Transparency Initiative in Albania Report for the year 2016*, Deloitte, http://www.deloitte.com/al/about. [12]

EITI (2019), *EITI Standard 2019*, Extractive Industries Transparency Initiative, Oslo, https://eiti.org/files/documents/eiti_standard_2019_en_a4_web.pdf. [3]

EITI (2019), *Feedback from Buying Companies on Reporting on Payments to EITI Countries*, Extractives Industries Transparency Initiative, Oslo. [30]

EITI (2017), *Guidance Note 26: Reporting on first trades in oil*, Extractives Industries Transparency Initiative, Oslo. [4]

FATF (2013), *Politically Exposed Persons (Recommendations 12 and 22)*, Financial Action Task Force, Paris, http://www.fatf-gafi.org. [32]

GHEITI (2018), *Ghana EITI Oil & Gas Commodity Trading Pilot*, Ghana Extractives Industries Transparency Initiative. [13]

Governing Board of the OECD Development Centre (2017), *Policy Statement on Natural Resource-based Development*, 4th High-level Meeting of the Governing Board, OECD Development Centre, Paris, https://www.oecd.org/dev/POLICY_STATEMENT_NATURAL_RESOURCES.pdf (accessed on 8 November 2020). [2]

IEITI (2016), *Extractive Industries Transparency Initiative in Iraq Report for the year 2015*, Iraq Extractive Industries Transparency Initiative. [23]

IISD/OECD (2018), *Monitoring the Value of Mineral Exports: Policy Options for Governments*, IGF-OECD Program to Address BEPS in Mining, https://www.oecd.org/tax/beps/monitoring-the-value-of-mineral-exports-policy-options-for-governments-oecd-igf.htm. [26]

Malden, A. and J. Williams (2019), *Big Sellers: Exploring the Scale and Risk of National Oil Company Sales*, Natural Resource Governance Institute, https://resourcegovernance.org/analysis-tools/publications/big-sellers-exploring-scale-and-risk-national-oil-company-sales. [1]

Mozambique Ministry of Energy and Mineral Resources (2016), *Terms of Reference: Public Tender - Natural Gas Project Development*, http://www.mireme.gov.mz. [25]

NNPC (2018), *Invitation to Tender for the Sale and Purchase of Nigerian Crude Oil Grades*, Nigerian National Petroleum Corporation, https://www.nnpcgroup.com/NNPCDocuments/Bids%20and%20Advert/NNPC%20Crude%20Advert%202018.pdf. [17]

OECD (2019), *Guidelines on Anti-Corruption and Integrity in State-Owned Enterprises*, OECD Publishing, Paris. [7]

OECD (2018), *State-Owned Enterprises and Corruption: What Are the Risks and What Can Be Done?*, OECD Publishing, Paris, https://doi.org/10.1787/9789264303058-en. [8]

OECD (2016), *Corruption in the Extractive Value Chain: Typology of Risks, Mitigation Measures and Incentives*, OECD Development Policy Tools, OECD Publishing, Paris, https://doi.org/10.1787/9789264256569-en. [6]

OECD (2015), *OECD Guidelines on Corporate Governance of State-Owned Enterprises, 2015 Edition*, OECD Publishing, Paris, https://dx.doi.org/10.1787/9789264244160-en. [9]

OECD (2009), *Guidelines for Fighting Bid Rigging in Public Procurement*, OECD Publishing, Paris. [20]

OECD (2009), *OECD Principles for Integrity in Public Procurement*, OECD Publishing, Paris, https://doi.org/10.1787/9789264056527-en. [19]

OECD (2005), "OECD Guidelines on Corporate Governance of State-owned Enterprises", in *Corporate Governance of State-Owned Enterprises: A Survey of OECD Countries*, OECD Publishing, Paris, https://doi.org/10.1787/9789264009431-10-en. [5]

OECD (2003), *Managing Conflict of Interest in the Public Service: OECD Guidelines and Overview*, OECD Publishing, Paris. [11]

OECD Development Centre (2019), "Summary Report of the Thirteenth Plenary Meeting of the Policy Dialogue on Natural Resource-based Development", OECD Development Centre, Paris. [27]

OECD Development Centre (2019), "Summary Report of the Twelfth Meeting of the Policy Dialogue on Natural Resource-based Development", OECD Development Centre, Paris. [22]

OECD Development Centre (2018), "Preliminary Stock-take of the Selection Procedures used by State-owned Enterprises to Select Buyers of Oil, Gas and Minerals", OECD Development Centre, Paris. [10]

OECD Development Centre (2018), "Summary Report of the Tenth Plenary Meeting of the Policy Dialogue on Natural Resource-based Development", OECD Development Centre, Paris. [18]

OECD/AfDB (2016), *Anti-Bribery Policy and Compliance Guidance for African Companies*, OECD/AfDB Joint Initiative to Support Business Integrity and Anti-bribery Efforts in Africa. [34]

Okavango Diamond Company (2019), *Terms and Conditions of Sale – Version: May 2019*, Okavango Diamond Company, https://www.odc.co.bw/privacy-policy. [21]

P.M.I.® Comercio Internacional, S.A. de C.V. (2018), *Políticas comerciales de petróleo crudo*, http://www.pmi.com.mx/Documents/Pol%C3%ADticas%20Comerciales%20de%20Petr%C3%B3leo%20Crudo.pdf. [29]

Public Eye (2017), *Oil and embezzlement: Public Eye reveals Gunvor's secrets in Congo*, Public Eye, https://www.publiceye.ch/en/media-corner/press-releases/detail/oil-and-embezzlement-public-eye-reveals-gunvors-secrets-in-congo/. [16]

RCS Global (2018), *Fact-Finding Report: The Sales of Minerals and Metals by Governments and State-Owned Enterprises: Scale, Nature and Disclosure Practices*, RCS Global. [28]

Sayne, A., A. Gillies and C. Katsouris (2015), *Inside NNPC Oil Sales: A Case for Reform in Nigeria*, Natural Resource Governance Institute. [15]

Sayne, A., A. Gillies and A. Watkins (2017), *Twelve Red Flags: Corruption Risks in the Award of Extractive Sector Licenses and Contracts*, Natural Resource Governance Institute. [24]

Van Schaik, J. (2012), *How Governments Sell Their Oil*, Revenue Watch Institute (RWI), http://www.revenuewatch.org/oilsales. [14]

Votava, C., J. Hauch and F. Clementucci (2018), *License to Drill A Manual on Integrity Due Diligence for Licensing in Extractive Sectors*, https://elibrary.worldbank.org/doi/abs/10.1596/978-1-4648-1271-2 (accessed on 16 November 2020). [31]

Westenberg, E. and A. Sayne (2018), *Beneficial Ownership Screening: Practical Measures to Reduce Corruption Risks in Extractives Licensing*, Natural Resource Governance Institute, https://resourcegovernance.org/sites/default/files/documents/beneficial-ownership-screening_0.pdf (accessed on 12 November 2020). [33]

www.ingramcontent.com/pod-product-compliance
Lightning Source LLC
LaVergne TN
LVHW061957070526
838199LV00060B/4175